St. Luke
425 East 38th St.
Erie, PA 16504

THE HISTORY OF THE **HOUSTON TEXANS**

THE HISTORY OF THE
HOUSTON

Published by Creative Education
123 South Broad Street
Mankato, Minnesota 56001
Creative Education is an imprint of The Creative Company.

DESIGN AND PRODUCTION BY **EVANSDAY DESIGN**

Copyright © 2005 Creative Education.
International copyright reserved in all countries.
No part of this book may be reproduced in any form
without written permission from the publisher.
Printed in the United States of America

LIBRARY OF CONGRESS CATALOGING-IN-PUBLICATION DATA

Nichols, John, 1966–
The history of the Houston Texans / by John Nichols.
p. cm. — (NFL today)
Summary: Traces the history of the team from its beginnings through 2003.
ISBN 1-58341-298-0
1. Houston Texans (Football team)—History—Juvenile literature.
[1. Houston Texans (Football team)—History. 2. Football—History.]
I. Title. II. Series.

GV956.H69N53 2004
796.332'64'097641411—dc22   2003065036

First edition

9 8 7 6 5 4 3 2 1

COVER PHOTO: quarterback David Carr

PHOTOGRAPHS BY
AP/Wide World Photos, Corbis (Reuters), Getty Images, SportsChrome USA

TEXANS

John Nichols

THE CITY OF **HOUSTON** IS LOCATED IN THE SOUTHEAST CORNER OF TEXAS ON THE SHORES OF THE GULF OF MEXICO. NAMED AFTER SAM HOUSTON, THE GENERAL WHO HELPED WIN TEXAS'S FREEDOM FROM MEXICO IN 1836, THE CITY HAS GROWN FROM A MUDDY LITTLE TOWN INTO THE FOURTH-LARGEST CITY IN THE UNITED STATES. HOUSTON'S RAPID GROWTH WAS SPURRED IN PART BY THE AREA'S ENORMOUS OIL WEALTH AND THE FACT THAT IT IS THE HEADQUARTERS OF THE NATIONAL AERONAUTICS AND SPACE ADMINISTRATION (NASA). THE PEOPLE OF HOUSTON, AND OF TEXAS AS A WHOLE, HAVE LONG LOVED FOOTBALL. FROM 1960 TO 1997, FANS TURNED OUT IN DROVES TO WATCH THE HOUSTON OILERS OF THE NATIONAL FOOTBALL LEAGUE (NFL). WHEN THE OILERS MOVED TO TENNESSEE IN 1997, FANS WERE CRUSHED. BUT IN 2002, THE NFL RETURNED TO HOUSTON IN THE FORM OF A NEW FRANCHISE. DECKED OUT IN UNIFORMS OF BLUE, RED, AND WHITE, THE CLUB WAS NAMED THE HOUSTON TEXANS.

[Running back James Allen]

A FRESH START IN HOUSTON>

ON APRIL 30, 1996, the NFL approved the Houston Oilers' move to Nashville, Tennessee, ending a streak of 37 seasons of professional football in Houston. Oilers owner Bud Adams declared that he could no longer compete financially playing in the aging Astrodome stadium. Houston fans were angered by the move, having supported the Oilers through thick and thin.

Realizing that the city was one of the finest football towns in the country, Houston businessman Robert McNair began discussions with the NFL in 1997 about bringing an expansion team to the city. NFL commissioner Paul Tagliabue praised McNair's efforts, and a plan began to take shape.

Robert McNair tried to bring an expansion hockey team to Houston before founding the Texans

Defensive tackle Gary Walker was a Pro-Bowler for the Jaguars the year before joining Houston.

Red 8! Red 8! Set! Hut!

In 1998, McNair met with Tagliabue and unveiled his group's plan to build a state-of-the-art, retractable-roof stadium to house a new team. The NFL was impressed with Houston's plan, and in October 1999, NFL owners voted 29–0 to award the league's 32nd franchise to Houston for a record price of $700 million. The team would be placed in the American Football Conference's (AFC) South Division and would begin play in 2002.

After using polls to gather input from Houston fans, McNair's group announced that the franchise would be named the Texans, and that its colors would be steel blue, battle red, and liberty white. "We realize that the people of Houston had their hearts broken when the Oilers moved," said McNair. "We want to make sure that they feel this team is all theirs from day one."

THE TEXANS COME TOGETHER>

TO BUILD HIS new team, McNair looked for an experienced general manager with an eye for talent and a coach who could get his players to jell quickly. In January 2000, Houston hired Charley Casserly as the team's general manager. Casserly had spent 10 years as the general manager of the Washington Redskins. Under his direction, the Redskins won three Super Bowl titles. "Charley is a bulldog," said New York Giants general manager George Young. "He gets his teeth into something and works hard at it."

The expansion Texans added speed and veteran leadership by signing cornerback Aaron Glenn.

Coach Dom Capers's combination of experience and enthusiasm made him a perfect fit in Houston

Crash 12 Crash 12! Set! Hut Hut!

Casserly's first move as general manager was to hire head coach Dom Capers. A detail-oriented coach known for his great defensive strategies, Capers had a history of success in building teams from scratch. In 1995, he had led the expansion Carolina Panthers to a 7–9 record, the best ever for a first-year NFL team. The very next season, Capers took the upstart Panthers all the way to the National Football Conference (NFC) championship game. "I know the type of work that's involved in building an expansion team," said Capers. "You have to work hard, have a plan, and not take shortcuts."

Capers joined the Texans in January 2001. His experience with the Panthers had taught him that the fastest way to build a winner was to start with a core of veteran leaders and work in promising young players around them. The Texans' first opportunity to acquire veteran talent came during an expansion draft held in February 2002. The 31 existing NFL teams were allowed to protect a certain number of players on their roster. Any players left unprotected could be selected by the Texans. Most of the players left unprotected were either inexperienced or past their prime, but Houston was able to grab several quality performers.

Linebacker Jamie Sharper met all expectations in 2002, leading the young Texans with 137 tackles

The biggest name was offensive tackle Tony Boselli of the Jacksonville Jaguars. Boselli had been a five-time Pro Bowler but had suffered a serious shoulder injury in 2001 that threatened his future. Houston gambled that Boselli would recover. Unfortunately, Boselli's shoulder would never fully heal, and he would retire without ever playing a down for the Texans.

Houston had better luck with other expansion picks such as rugged defensive tackles Gary Walker and Seth Payne, swift cornerbacks Aaron Glenn and Marcus Coleman, and linebacker Jamie Sharper. Casserly and Capers made sure to choose players who were still in their prime and showed strong leadership skills. "We know that there will be some tough times ahead," said Sharper, a starter on the Baltimore Ravens Super Bowl championship team in 2000. "We have to be strong for the young guys."

Down! Line 15 Set! Hut Hut!

A LUXURY CARR >

AFTER THE EXPANSION draft, the Texans had only a few weeks to prepare for the NFL Draft, in which teams select college players. Luckily, the team knew exactly who it wanted to choose with the number one overall pick: quarterback David Carr from Fresno State University. Carr had been a college superstar, throwing for 42 touchdowns and more than 4,000 yards his senior season. The 6-foot-3 and 230-pound passer had all the physical tools to be a great NFL quarterback—a cannon of an arm, quick feet, and great field vision.

During his college career, Carr had helped turn Fresno State from a doormat into a nationally ranked team. The shining moment in his college career may have been his final game, in which he completed 35 of 56 passes for an incredible 531 yards and five touchdowns in a 44–35 loss to Michigan State University.

Rookie quarterback David Carr led the first-year Texans with the poise and toughness of a veteran.

Top passing target Corey Bradford showed his speed in 2002, taking one pass reception 81 yards

Orange 18 Orange 18! Set! Hut!

Texans fans expected big things from Jabar Gaffney

Kailee Wong added quickness to Houston's defense

After selecting Carr, the Texans showed their commitment by flying him directly from the draft site in New York to Houston, where he signed a seven-year contract. The Texans were counting on the young man from Bakersfield, California, to become the cornerstone of the franchise. "David doesn't have to be Superman," said Coach Capers. "He just has to be David Carr."

After taking Carr, Houston plucked some other promising offensive players from the 2002 NFL Draft. Speedy wide receiver Jabar Gaffney from the University of Florida gave Carr an inviting passing target, while powerful offensive linemen Chester Pitts and Fred Weary were selected to protect the young quarterback.

The Texans also found some firepower in the free-agent market, signing big-play receiver Corey Bradford from the Green Bay Packers, center Steve McKinney from the Indianapolis Colts, and linebackers Kailee Wong and Jay Foreman from the Minnesota Vikings and Buffalo Bills, respectively. With the team finally assembled, it was time for the dream that was the Houston Texans to finally become reality.

Down! Black 19 Set! Hut!

THE TEXANS STAND TALL>

ONE ADVANTAGE THE Texans had working for them was beautiful new Reliant Stadium. Named after the facility's corporate sponsor, Reliant Energy, the 69,500-seat stadium was the first in the NFL to have a retractable roof. During extremely hot or stormy weather, the roof could be closed within 10 minutes. On pleasant days, the roof would be opened so fans could enjoy the fresh air.

With the retractable roof and access to sunshine, Reliant Stadium did not have to use artificial turf like other domed facilities. Instead, the field featured beautifully groomed, natural grass. "I've never played on anything like it," said Texans safety Eric Brown. "The grass is easy on your body, and the fans here are right on top of you."

Hard-hitting safety Eric Brown proved to be a valuable addition, intercepting two passes in 2002.

The Texans' first opponent in Reliant Stadium was a familiar one to Houston fans. The five-time Super Bowl champion Dallas Cowboys—known to their fans as "America's Team"—would be the first to tangle with the Texans. The Cowboys had long been the dominant football franchise in Texas. Even during the Oilers' finest seasons, the Cowboys still overshadowed their southern neighbors. For the Cowboys, the game was an opportunity to squash the upstart Texans and put them in their place. For the Texans, the game was a chance to make clear that Texas was not exclusively Cowboys country anymore.

After receiving the opening kickoff, the Texans wasted little time in scoring their first touchdown. On the third play from scrimmage, Carr zipped a 19-yard touchdown pass to tight end Billy Miller. Dallas fought back to tie the game 10–10, but Carr untied the contest with a 65-yard touchdown bomb to a streaking Corey Bradford. Houston's defense kept Dallas bottled up and added a safety late in the game to secure a 19–10 Texans victory. Houston became the first expansion team to win its opening game since the 1961 Minnesota Vikings. "I don't know what the rest of the season holds," said Houston running back James Allen, "but this win will be remembered for a long, long time."

Quick and sure-handed halfback James Allen contributed 821 total yards to Houston's offense in 2002.

Tight end Billy Miller secured a special place in Texans history by scoring the franchise's first touchdown

Dog 24! Dog 24! Set! Hut Hut!

The scrappy Texans played hard throughout the 2002 season. The high points were kicker Kris Brown's late 45-yard field goal to clinch Houston's first road win (a 21–19 victory over the Jacksonville Jaguars), a 16–14 win over the playoff-bound New York Giants, and a 24–6 win over the Pittsburgh Steelers that featured two long interception returns for touchdowns by Aaron Glenn.

Houston finished its first season with a 4–12 record. Individually, Glenn's five interceptions and Gary Walker's seven quarterback sacks earned them each Pro Bowl honors. Carr played admirably, especially considering the young quarterback was sacked 76 times, a new single-season NFL record. "People wondered if David had the guts to take the pressure of being a starter in the NFL," said Coach Capers. "He got knocked around a lot this year, but he never flinched. He's the real deal."

DRIVING FOR A TEXAS TITLE>

BEFORE THE 2003 season, Houston concentrated on surrounding Carr with better blockers and more talented receivers and runners. The team found one talented offensive lineman on the free-agent market, signing massive tackle Zach Wiegert from the Jacksonville Jaguars. The 6-foot-5 and 310-pound Wiegert had established himself as a pass-blocking force during his eight seasons in the league.

Then, in the 2003 NFL Draft, Houston selected receiver Andre Johnson in the first round, bruising tight end Bennie Joppru in the second round, and speedy linebacker Antwan Peek in the third round. The 6-foot-2 and 220-pound Johnson possessed a rare combination of speed and strength. During his final college season, he averaged an amazing 21 yards per reception. His addition gave Carr a big target who had the potential to score

Andre Johnson lived up to the hype by posting almost 1,000 receiving yards in his rookie season

every time he touched the ball. "Andre is a special talent," said Carr. "I look forward to being a part of a lot of great plays with him."

The Texans also used the NFL Draft to nab speedy running back Tony Hollings. Hollings had gotten off to an explosive start in his last college season at Georgia Tech, gaining more than 600 yards and scoring 11 touchdowns in just four games. A knee injury ended that season, but his brilliant performance and star potential caught the eye of Houston talent scouts. "We think Tony can be an impact back for us," said Capers. "He has all the tools."

The Texans entered the 2003 season hoping to show improvement on the field and in the standings. The team got off to another quick start, upsetting the heavily favored Miami Dolphins 21–20 on the road in the season opener. Another highlight came three weeks later in Reliant Stadium when the Texans beat the Jacksonville Jaguars 24–20. The victory was sealed on the final play of the game as Carr made a one-yard touchdown dive over a pile of players. That exciting victory had Houston fans dreaming of a winning season, but the dream quickly faded when Carr and defensive standouts Gary Walker and Seth Payne were sidelined with injuries.

Young rusher Domanick Davis proved tough to bring down during his surprising 2003 season

Although Houston finished its second season just 5–11, several players showed flashes of stardom. With Tony Hollings still slowed by his knee injury, Domanick Davis—a running back from Louisiana State University picked up in the fourth round of the 2003 NFL Draft—stepped into the lineup and rushed for 1,031 yards. Andre Johnson caught 66 passes for 976 yards, and veteran cornerback Marcus Coleman snared seven interceptions. "Through good times and bad, our guys never quit this year," said a proud Coach Capers. "We took another step toward our goal of building a winner in Houston."

In just a few short years, the people of Houston have cast off the memories of the departed Oilers and embraced a new team built from scratch. The young Texans know that the journey toward an NFL championship may be long and hard, but after their first two seasons, they seem to be well on their way. In a city named after one of Texas's first heroes, Houston fans will long be cheering for this new generation of football heroes.

The Texans hoped that a healthy Tony Hollings would help them continue to climb up the standings.

INDEX>

A

Adams, Bud 6
Allen, James 5, 22, 22–23
Astrodome 6

B

Boselli, Tony 15
Bradford, Corey 18, 19, 22
Brown, Eric 20, 21
Brown, Kris 25

C

Capers, Dom 12–13, 13, 15, 19, 25, 28, 30
Carr, David 16, 17, 19, 22, 25, 26, 28
Casserly, Charley 10, 13, 15
Coleman, Marcus 15, 30

D

Davis, Domanick 28–29, 30

E

expansion draft 13, 15, 16

F

Foreman, Jay 19

G

Gaffney, Jabar 19, 19
Glenn, Aaron 11, 15, 25

H

Hollings, Tony 28, 30, 30–31
Houston Oilers 4, 6, 9, 22, 30

J

Johnson, Andre 26, 27, 30
Joppru, Bennie 26

M

McKinney, Steve 19
McNair, Robert 6, 7, 9, 10
Miller, Billy 22, 24–25

N

NFL records 25

P

Payne, Seth 15, 28
Peek, Antwan 26
Pitts, Chester 19

R

Reliant Stadium 20, 22, 28

S

Sharper, Jamie 14–15, 15

T

Tagliabue, Paul 6, 9
Texans name 9

W

Walker, Gary 8, 8–9, 15, 28
Weary, Fred 19
Wiegert, Zach 26
Wong, Kailee 19, 19